better together*

*This book is best read together, grownup and kid.

akidsco.com

a kids book about

a kids book about overdose

by Lee S. Varon, LICSW

a kids book about

Text and design copyright © 2024
by A Kids Book About, Inc.

Copyright is good! It ensures that work like this can exist, and more work in the future can be created.

All rights reserved. No part of this publication may be reproduced, distributed, or transmitted in any form or by any means, including photocopying, recording, other electronic or mechanical methods, without the prior written permission of the publisher, except in the case of brief quotations embodied in critical reviews and certain other noncommercial uses permitted by copyright law. For permission requests, write to the publisher.

A Kids Book About, Kids Are Ready, and the colophon 'a' are trademarks of A Kids Book About, Inc.

Printed in the United States of America.

A Kids Book About books are available online: *akidsco.com*

To share your stories, ask questions, or inquire about bulk purchases (schools, libraries, and nonprofits), please use the following email address: *hello@akidsco.com*

Print ISBN: 979-8-89281-068-5
Ebook ISBN: 979-8-89281-069-2

Designed by Jelani Memory
Edited by Emma Wolf

This book is dedicated, with love and gratitude to my sons, Jose and Jude.

Important Information

MEDICAL DISCLAIMER: The information and story in this book represent the personal experience and opinion of the author, are for informational purposes only, are not medical advice, and are not a substitute for professional medical advice, diagnosis, or treatment.

Always seek the advice of your physician or other qualified healthcare provider with any questions you may have regarding a medical condition or treatment and before undertaking new healthcare or emergency healthcare treatments, and never disregard professional medical advice or delay in seeking it because of something you have read in this book.

Intro

It can be frightening when you hear the word *overdose*. Especially if someone you know or love has experienced an overdose. Your impulse might be to protect kids from this topic. But not talking about it may increase their confusion, worry, and anxiety.

Many kids have heard of an overdose and have questions about it. When dealing with any difficult subject, it is much easier for kids when they have a caring grownup, who loves and supports them, to listen and help them make sense of things. This book can help!

We don't have to know all the answers to begin a conversation. *A Kids Book About Overdose* offers concise and factual information that can help kids and grownups discuss this topic. What is an overdose? What might we be asked to do if someone near us experiences an overdose? What steps can we discuss with medical professionals to help keep ourselves and others safe?

Let's dive into this together.

Do you know what an overdose is?

Simply put, it's when you have too much of something.

Have you ever heard someone say, "I overdosed on chocolate!"?

They probably have a stomachache now!

But this book isn't about that kind of overdose.

This is a book about when someone **overdoses on a drug or medicine**.

This is a very serious topic, so I'm proud of you for joining me.

First of all, I want you to know there are 2 kinds of drugs that can cause an

dose.

The first

is a legal kind of drug.

Usually, people are prescribed* these medications by their doctors or healthcare providers, and they are available to be picked up at the pharmacy.

They have names like Vicodin, OxyContin, fentanyl, and Percocet.

*In medicine, "prescribe" means to order the use of a medicine or treatment, usually by a doctor or healthcare provider.

The second

kind of drug is illegal (or, not legal).

Illegal drugs are not prescribed by a doctor, and they aren't meant for any person to take.

Why would someone take medication that isn't meant for them?

Sometimes, people are curious about how they'll feel when they take drugs.

But when you take something that isn't prescribed by a doctor and isn't meant for you, dangerous things can happen.

Sometimes, a pill may look exactly like something a doctor prescribes, but it is a counterfeit* and could contain some very bad ingredients.

*Have you heard of a counterfeit dollar bill? It can look exactly like a real dollar bill, but it's actually fake. Drugs can also be fake, or counterfeit. When they are, they can be deadly.

And regardless of whether a drug is legal or illegal, it can cause an overdose or addiction.

Being addicted to something means a person needs that thing just to feel OK throughout the day.

But if they suddenly stop taking a drug they're addicted to, they'll feel really bad.

Some people who overdose on a drug have an addiction, also called a substance use disorder (SUD).

Addiction is a disease, and it's really hard on the person with the addiction and all the people who care for them.

But addiction can be treated, and people with an addiction can get better.

And not everyone who overdoses has the disease of addiction.

When someone is given medication from a doctor, unless they take it exactly as prescribed, they can be at risk of addiction or an overdose.

This probably sounds scary.

I want you to know, being able to receive medicine from a doctor when you really need it is a good thing.

That's why

it exists!

But medicine is powerful, and it requires care, attention, and responsibility.

Maybe you're wondering what happens when someone overdoses.

It can look different depending on the kind of drug someone took.

The most common types of overdoses are from drugs called opioids, and here are some of the symptoms:

Slowed breathing, or no breathing at all.

Throwing up.

Choking.

Blue or purple lips and fingertips.

No response to loudly calling the person's name, or rubbing your knuckles on the center of their chest.

Looking like they're sleeping.

I hope you never see someone experiencing an overdose.

It's a really scary thing for anyone, kid or grownup.

what cou

But, if someone sees someone else experiencing an overdose, **ld they do?**

Get help from a grownup **IMMEDIATELY!**

From a phone, dial 911.

Tell the operator that they are with a person who can't wake up.

Stay on the phone and follow their instructions **EXACTLY**.

2.

The 911 operator will ask them questions to understand if the person is in danger because of an overdose.

The operator may ask them if they have access to naloxone* nasal spray.

*Naloxone (brand name, Narcan) is a lifesaving medicine that can reverse the effects of an opioid overdose. It is available over the counter as a nasal spray and in injectable form by prescription. It is important that a trusted grownup has demonstrated how to use it before anyone attempts to administer it to someone else.

While the emergency team is on their way, the 911 operator may ask them to administer the naloxone nasal spray to the person who needs it.

The instructions may be to tilt the person's head back and carefully spray the naloxone into 1 nostril.

2 CONT.

It is important they stay on the phone, keep watching, and let the operator know if the person is not responding.

After 2-3 minutes, they may be asked to carefully spray the naloxone into the other nostril of the person who needs help.*

*The use of naloxone is **never** a substitue for getting emergency medical treatment.

3.

They will be asked to follow the directions given by the 911 operator, regardless of whether naloxone has been administered.

It is important that they

stay calm,

speak clearly,

and never put themselves in danger.

They will be asked to stay with the person until help arrives.

If a person isn't treated immediately, they can die from an overdose.

But when treatment is provided immediately, many people won't die, and they can get help.

If the person has the disease of addiction, they may go to a treatment center for a while to get help.

Now, I know this conversation is really heavy.

But it's important to talk about these things so we can be aware and protect ourselves and those around us.

If someone other than a trusted grownup gives you a pill, do not take it.

Some fake and dangerous pills may look just like the ones which have been prescribed for you.

You may have a lot of mixed feelings if you know someone who has suffered an overdose.

Feelings like...

SCARED

ANGRY

SAD

CONFUSED

GUILTY

ANXIOUS

All of these feelings (and whatever else you're experiencing) are

nor

mal,
and it's OK to feel them.

We're almost done here, but there are 3 important things I want you to know.

They're based on something called the 3 C's.

1. You did not **Cause** the person's overdose.

2. You can't **Control** whether a person overdoses.

3. You can't **Cure** the person if they suffer from the disease of addiction which caused them to overdose.

Now, let's take a deep breath.

You just finished a book about a very difficult subject, and I'm really proud of you.

An overdose is a **scary thing.**

But I hope you (now) know that talking about scary things can make them feel

easier to

manage.

Outro

Thanks for being brave enough to read this book. I hope this is just the beginning of the conversation. I want you and the kid(s) in your life to feel empowered to open a new channel of communication where things like overdose can be addressed in a calm, clear, and proactive way.

ADDITIONAL SUGGESTIONS:

1. Keep all medications in a safe and secure place, and properly dispose of them when they are expired or no longer needed.

2. Keep a list of emergency contacts and make sure your kids know whom to call and what to say if they need to make an emergency call. Role-playing this can help.

3. If anyone in your home, or anyone you know, may be using opioids, have naloxone available and make sure everyone in your home knows how to use it.

4. Talking to your kid about an overdose will not cause them to use drugs. Not talking to them about an overdose could leave them confused and unprepared if an overdose happens.

About The Author

Lee S. Varon (she/her) worked as a social worker for many years, but it wasn't until addiction came to her own family that her real education in the field of substance use disorder began. Over several decades, she attended parent education seminars, read everything she could about the topic, and was in many support groups for families dealing with alcohol and drug use. These groups became a lifeline through years of fear, worry, exhaustion, and confusion as Lee dealt with her own child's addiction.

Today, that child is an adult and is in recovery. Lee wrote *A Kids Book About Overdose* to support, educate, and encourage other families going through similar experiences.

 @leesvaron    leesvaron.com

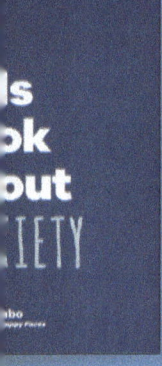

Discover more at akidsco.com